ABOUT
THIS AND THAT

PUBLISHER	Joseph R. DeVarennes
PUBLICATION DIRECTOR	Kenneth H. Pearson
ADVISORS	Roger Aubin
	Robert Furlonger
EDITORIAL SUPERVISOR	Jocelyn Smyth
PRODUCTION MANAGER	Ernest Homewood
PRODUCTION ASSISTANTS	Martine Gingras Kathy Kishimoto
	Catherine Gordon Peter Thomlison
CONTRIBUTORS	Alison Dickie Nancy Prasad
	Bill Ivy Lois Rock
	Jacqueline Kendel Merebeth Switzer
	Anne Langdon Dave Taylor
	Sheila Macdonald Alison Tharen
	Susan Marshall Donna Thomson
	Pamela Martin Pam Young
	Colin McCance
SENIOR EDITOR	Robin Rivers
EDITORS	Brian Cross Ann Martin
	Anne Louise Mahoney Mayta Tannenbaum
PUBLICATION ADMINISTRATOR	Anna Good
ART AND DESIGN	Richard Comely Ronald Migliore
	Robert B. Curry Penelope Moir
	George Elliott Marion Stuck
	Marilyn James Bill Suddick
	Robert Johanssen Sue Wilkinson

Canadian Cataloguing in Publication Data

Main entry under title:

Questions kids ask about this and that

(Questions kids ask; 27)
ISBN 0-7172-2566-6

1. Children's questions and answers.
I. Smyth, Jocelyn.   II. Comely, Richard.   III. Series.

AG195.Q48 1988   j031'.02   C89-093176-3

Questions Kids Ask... about THIS & THAT

continued

How old is the Earth?

Try to guess the Earth's age. Go on, try. What do you think? One thousand, one million, maybe even one billion years old? Scientists think that the Earth is probably at least 4 1/2 billion years old! That's 4 500 000 000 years. What a lot of candles for a birthday cake!

Scientists are still trying to unravel the secret of how the Earth was formed. Most scientists believe that the solar system developed from a huge cloud of gas and dust that once swirled around the sun. As the cloud whirled it slowly flattened out, and sections of it began to spin like whirlpools in a stream. Gas and dust collected near the center of the whirlpools. Slowly the gas and dust formed into balls, which grew larger and larger and eventually developed into the Earth and the other planets that now circle the sun.

Who invented breakfast cereal?

Many of us start each day with a bowl of cereal. But before the mid 1800s, nobody ate dry, ready-to-eat cereal because it hadn't been invented.

The first dry cereal was made at a hospital in Battle Creek, Michigan, in the 1860s, by grinding up and rebaking sheets of thin bread. A patient at the hospital named C.W. Post liked the cereal so much, he invented his own. W.K. Kellogg, who had also eaten and liked the cereal, invented another version. Post and Kellogg each started a company to manufacture, package and sell the cereal.

In 1906, Kellogg started the Battle Creek Toasted Corn Flake Company. It is now the world's largest manufacturer of dry cereals, and Battle Creek, Michigan, is the breakfast-cereal capital of the world.

SIGH

How do tins preserve food?

The air is full of tiny molds and bacteria that grow on food and cause it to go bad. These organisms grow faster when heat, light and moisture are present.

Refrigeration slows down food spoilage, but doesn't stop it. Canning was invented to keep food from spoiling. Meat, beans, soup, vegetables and fruit are processed in canning factories.

They are cooked at a high enough temperature to destroy any mold or bacteria already present in the food. Often they are cooked under pressure or vacuum-packed to keep out light and air.

Once opened, the food should be eaten right away since it is now exposed to mold organisms in the air and may start spoiling.

What is the fastest sport on earth?

There are many fast sports, such as autocar racing, bobsledding and hockey. But most people agree that the fastest sport that uses no special equipment is jai alai.

Jai alai is a sport that is very popular in Cuba, Mexico, South America, China and many European countries. It is a game that only needs two players, a wall, a ball and two "cestas."

A cesta is a long, narrow, curved wicker basket. Each player has a cesta strapped to one hand. The players catch the ball, which is a little smaller than a baseball, in the cestas. Then they use them to hurl the ball back at the wall.

The ball can travel at over 240 kilometres (150 miles) per hour —more than twice as fast as a car travels on the highway!

DID YOU KNOW . . . the slowest sport was amateur wrestling before the rules were modified. A single bout once lasted 11 hours and 40 minutes.

When was bowling invented?

Bowling is one of the oldest sports in the world, but no one knows exactly when it began. It has existed in one form or another for at least 7000 years. Archaeologists in Egypt found equipment for a bowling type of game buried with a child in 5200 B.C.

Different countries have had different rules and have played with different sized balls but people everywhere have loved this sport. Even the ancient Polynesians bowled, and in the Middle Ages in Europe, people bowled to celebrate special occasions. Bowling is the most popular sport in North America.

DID YOU KNOW . . . bowling was banned in England in the 1100s. Too many people were bowling and not enough were practising archery—a sport upon which the defense of the country depended.

Who scored the most runs in one inning?

Can you imagine scoring 337 runs for your team in one inning? That's just what Hanif Mahammad of Pakistan did in 1958 when he came to bat in a cricket match in Bridgetown, Barbados.

In cricket, the batsman stays up as long as he can protect the wicket and none of the balls he hits are caught. Hanif managed to do this for 16 hours and 10 minutes while he racked up his phenomenal number of runs. The inning was played over three days.

The ticket-holders to that game sure got their money's worth!

What is a saga?

Originally, a saga was an exciting story or group of stories told in Iceland and Norway during the Middle Ages. The people who told the stories were called sagamen. They traveled around and received rewards in return for telling their stories. Sagas were usually based on fact, and were often violent and filled with suspense.

Some sagas, such as *The Icelandic Sagas,* gave detailed histories of the fortunes of the great Icelandic families. Others, such as *The First Saga of King Olaf,* recounted the adventures and accomplishments of kings and royalty.

Today, a saga means a story that has the characteristics of the Icelandic sagas: heroic achievement, marvelous adventures or a long family history.

What is sand?

Have you ever wondered where sand comes from? Sand is formed when the force of wind or water breaks large rocks into smaller and smaller pieces. This is called *erosion*. Erosion is a slow process—it takes thousands of years to create the sand on a beach.

How long can camels go without water?

It depends. During the six or seven cool months in the Sahara Desert, camels do not usually drink. They get enough water from the plants they eat. When the temperature rises to 35°C (95°F), a camel will go about 15 days between drinks. However, when the temperature hits 40°C (104°F) a camel will drink as often as it can.

DID YOU KNOW . . . a thirsty camel may drink 135 litres (just over 135 quarts) of water in just a few minutes.

Who was Pocahontas?

Daughter of North American Indian Chief Powhatan, Pocahontas befriended the early settlers in Virginia. She risked her life to save Captain John Smith, the leader of the settlers of the Jamestown colony, who was captured by Indian warriors. She also was known to bring the settlers food to keep them from starving. The kindness of Pocahontas helped the young Virginia colony to grow.

She went to live in Jamestown and learned the English way of life. By marrying a settler, Pocahontas assisted in creating an eight-year period of peace between the Indians and settlers. She traveled to England with her family and a group of Indians, where she visited the royal palace. While in England, Pocahontas died of smallpox.

sharpshooter she starred in Buffalo Bill's Wild West Show for 17 years, touring North America and Europe.

Born Phoebe Anne Oakley Mozee in a log cabin in Ohio on August 13, 1860, she began shooting at the age of nine. When her father died several years later, Annie supported her family on the small game she hunted. Her expert marksmanship was legendary. Once, at his invitation, she shot a cigarette right out of the mouth of the German Crown Prince (later Wilhelm II).

Who was Annie Oakley?

Can you imagine being able to shoot glass balls right out of the air, or shooting a playing card in the air five or six times before it hit the ground? Well, Annie Oakley could do both of these things.

Nicknamed "Little Sure Shot," she was only 150 centimetres (5 feet) tall and one of the world's best shots—with a pistol, rifle and shotgun. As a

DID YOU KNOW . . . the musical *Annie Get Your Gun* is based on Annie Oakley's life.

Are there really Pygmies?

Pygmies are not just legend. They are real people. Many of them live in the Ituri Forest of the Zaire basin in central Africa.

The Pygmies' small size sets them apart from other African tribes. They rarely grow more than 150 centimetres (5 feet) tall, and many are shorter than that.

Most Pygmies live in small tribes of from 10 to 25 families. Their lives have changed very little over the centuries. They gather fruits and vegetables, and hunt with nets, spears, and bows and arrows. They live in simple beehive-shaped huts made of sticks and covered with leaves. About once a month, when they have eaten much of the food in an area, they abandon their camp and move on.

The Pygmies celebrate important occasions with singing dancing, and mime. Their music is known for its complex rhythms and harmonies.

Are carrots good for your eyes?

Yes!

Carrots contain a lot of Vitamin A, which helps your eyes to work their best. If you aren't getting enough Vitamin A, you will notice it at night right away. People with healthy eyes can see shapes and shadows quite well in the dark, but people lacking in Vitamin A cannot. This condition is called night blindness.

But what if you don't like carrots? Don't worry, there are other foods that have plenty of Vitamin A: dried apricots, cheddar cheese, broccoli, tomatoes and . . . liver.

DID YOU KNOW . . . in some places, carrots are roasted and ground and used instead of coffee.

What are marshmallows?

We think of marshmallows as a treat to roast around a campfire. But at times when other food ran out, marsh mallow roots were all some people had to eat.

What is a marsh mallow? It is a plant that grows in the swamps and marshes of eastern Europe. The root of this plant is white and shaped like a carrot. At one time these roots were used in making the white marshmallow candy we know.

The name has lasted although the ingredients have changed. Today, syrup, gelatin, egg whites, and sugar are beaten together very quickly to get air into the mixture. This trapped air makes marshmallows light and fluffy and easy to chew.

What is a labyrinth?

A labyrinth is a maze of narrow pathways with high walls that cross each other, and only one path leads to the center.

In Greek mythology, King Minos kept a monster, the Minotaur, in a very confusing labyrinth.

Every year seven young men and seven young women from Athens were given to Minos. He sent them into the labyrinth to be killed by the Minotaur.

One year an Athenian prince decided to try to kill the Minotaur. Minos' daughter gave him a magic sword and a spool of thread to help him. He killed the Minotaur, followed the trail he had made with the thread, and escaped the labyrinth.

What is the food of the gods?

Greek and Roman gods and goddesses never grew old and died because they ate a food called ambrosia that kept them young and strong. Every day, pigeons brought ambrosia to Mount Olympus, the home of the gods. They ate this magical substance, bathed in it or rubbed it on their skin. This made sure they remained immortal, or lived forever. A human who ate or drank ambrosia became strong, beautiful and immortal.

Why was Louis XIV called "the Sun King"?

Just as the planets revolve around the sun, King Louis XIV insisted that everything revolve around himself. That's why he was called "the Sun King." He ruled France from 1643 to 1715, the longest reign in European history. Louis wanted to decide everything on his own. He ignored advice from advisors on economic and war strategies, religious and artistic policies. He wanted absolute power and was so bold as to declare "I am the state." He fought wars with most of the other European countries and enlarged his country. He also strengthened it against attack.

He sought to glorify the crown and France. The Sun King built a new palace at Versailles, and all the roads left the palace in a pattern like the sun's rays. He attracted nobles to his glittering court so they would not plot against him elsewhere. But the huge amount of money he spent and the numerous wars he fought made him very unpopular by the time of his death.

DID YOU KNOW . . . Louis XIV became king when he was four years old.

22

Who was Attila the Hun?

The Huns were nomads, or wanderers, from Asia who conquered much of Europe in the fourth century. In 433, Attila and his brother Bleda became kings of the Huns. Attila later murdered his brother so he could become the sole leader.

He wanted to conquer the Roman Empire. To keep him away the Romans paid him 300 kilograms (700 pounds) of gold every year. Attila expanded his empire to the north and the east and kept peace with Rome for six years. Then he invaded several Roman cities. He stopped when the annual payment of gold was raised to 900 kilograms (2000 pounds). Then he started invading western Europe.

In 452, Attila invaded Italy, intending to capture Rome itself. The campaign failed. Disease killed many of his men and Attila was forced to withdraw. The invasion proved to be Attila's last. A year later he was dead—some say he was murdered. Lacking a strong leader, the great Hun empire soon collapsed.

What were the seven wonders of the world?

The seven wonders of the ancient world were beautiful works of art created more than 2000 years ago. Only one of these, the Pyramids of Egypt, remains—but archaeological finds and ancient writings tell us how the rest must have looked. Were they really wonders? You be the judge.

The Pyramids of Egypt are the oldest of the seven ancient wonders. One of them, the Great Pyramid at Giza, was built from 2 1/2 million limestone blocks fitted so tightly together that you can barely see any spaces between them. And it was all built without machines to help do the work.

The Hanging Gardens of Babylon were built in Mesopotamia (near modern Baghdad in Iraq). The gardens were planted on a brick terrace about 120 metres (400 feet) square and 25 metres (80 feet) above the ground. The thousands of trees and flowers planted there looked as if they were floating in the air from a distance.

The Colossus of Rhodes was a huge bronze statue that stood in the harbor of the island of Rhodes near Turkey. It stood about 37 metres (120 feet) tall. That's about 20 times the height of a tall adult!

The Temple of Artemis at Ephesus was built to honor the

Greek goddess Artemis. It was one of the largest temples built in ancient times and took up more space than a football field. And the entire temple (except the roof) was built from white marble!

The Pharos of Alexandria was built on Egypt's Mediterranean coast. It was a gigantic lighthouse about 135 metres (440 feet) high. The light was given off by roaring fires, which were kept burning night and day and reflected (probably by a metal mirror) far across the Mediterranean Sea. For 1000 years, its fire helped to guide ships safely into the harbor.

The Mausoleum of Halicarnassus was a huge marble tomb built for King Mausolos of Caria. It was about 40 metres (135 feet) high, had a colonnade formed by 36 towering columns, and was topped by a statue of the king in his chariot. Because of it all large tombs are now called mausoleums.

The Statue of Zeus at Olympia, Greece, was probably the most famous statue in the ancient world. It stood 12 metres (40 feet) high. Zeus's skin was carved from ivory, his clothes and ornaments from gold, and his eyes from large precious jewels!

What are gargoyles?

During the Middle Ages, drainage spouts were added to stone buildings. Water ran down from rain gutters on the roof to these spouts, or gargoyles. The gargoyles stuck out from the walls, allowing water to fall away from the building instead of seeping through the stone. When water drips on stone over a long period of time, the stone begins to wear down, or erode.

At first, gargoyles were just plain pieces of stone. Soon artists began carving faces resembling those of humans, birds and animals. The water drained out of the mouth of the figures. Often the gargoyles looked scary, perhaps to frighten away evil spirits. After the lead drain pipe was introduced in the 1700s, gargoyles were no longer needed as water spouts. They were used for decoration.

DID YOU KNOW . . .
the Greek god Zeus made the first cornucopia from a goat's horn. He used his special powers to make the horn always full of food and drink.

What is a cornucopia?

What do you think of when you think of Thanksgiving? Do you picture falling leaves, a big turkey with cranberry sauce and pumpkin pie with whipped cream? Do you also think of a strange basket shaped like a goat's horn?

Well, many people use a cornucopia, or horn of plenty, at Thanksgiving. They fill it with fruit, vegetables and flowers to represent a good harvest.

What is a ghost?

How many times have you been told, "There is no such thing as a ghost"? Probably too often. But what about people who claim they have seen a ghost? They must have seen something—but what?

Parapsychologists are scientists who are interested in finding the answer. According to their observations, ghosts are life forces left over from a person who died which may linger on for up to 400 years. No ghost has ever harmed anyone. In fact, most ghosts don't seem to be aware of people at all.

Many people believe that all ghost sightings are nothing more than figments of the imagination. It is true that the eyes and mind can easily be fooled into seeing something that's not there . . . just ask any magician!

Where is Davy Jones' locker?

A locker is a place where you store things. It has a door with a lock and key. Davy Jones' locker is huge and it has no door or lock or key. Where is it? At the bottom of the sea!

To sailors, the sea has moods and emotions just like a person. It can be calm and peaceful, or angry and turbulent. No one knows exactly why or when sailors began calling the spirit, or personality of the sea, Davy Jones. When people drowned or were buried at sea, sailors said their bodies went to Davy Jones' locker—the bottom of the sea.

Perhaps the expression arose because sailors were very superstitious. They wouldn't say the word ''drown'' because that might make a drowning happen.

DID YOU KNOW . . . while the bodies of sailors who drown or are buried at sea go to Davy Jones' locker, their souls go to Fiddler's Green, sailors' heaven.

Can plants take away pain?

Plants have been used to treat illness and disease for over 4500 years. Chemicals in the roots, stems, leaves, flowers or fruit of many plants can be used as medicine.

Antibiotics, which destroy bacteria, are made from plant mold. Bark from the willow tree can be used as a pain reliever. Morphine, a strong pain-killer, is made from the poppy plant. Digitalis, made from dried foxglove leaves, is used to treat heart disease. The number of medicinal plants increases as new plants are discovered.

But be careful before you make medicine out of a plant—although many plants can help you get well, others can make you sick.

What is an iceberg?

When a glacier (a huge mass of ice that moves across land) reaches the sea, large chunks of it break off and fall into the water. This is how icebergs are created. An iceberg may be 120 metres (400 feet) high—and that's only the part that's above water! Scientists estimate that the part you can see is only one-tenth of the total iceberg. Lurking underwater is the rest—up to another kilometre (3600 feet) of ice.

Icebergs from the north drift south into warmer waters where they break up into smaller and smaller pieces, then finally melt altogether, somewhere between the North Pole and the equator.

Index